Learning to Read, Step by Step!

Ready to Read   Preschool–Kindergarten
• big type and easy words • rhyme and rhythm • picture clues
For children who know the alphabet and are eager to begin reading.

Reading with Help   Preschool–Grade 1
• basic vocabulary • short sentences • simple stories
For children who recognize familiar words and sound out new words with help.

Reading on Your Own   Grades 1–3
• engaging characters • easy-to-follow plots • popular topics
For children who are ready to read on their own.

Reading Paragraphs   Grades 2–3
• challenging vocabulary • short paragraphs • exciting stories
For newly independent readers who read simple sentences with confidence.

Ready for Chapters   Grades 2–4
• chapters • longer paragraphs • full-color art
For children who want to take the plunge into chapter books but still like colorful pictures.

STEP INTO READING® is designed to give every child a successful reading experience. The grade levels are only guides; children will progress through the steps at their own speed, developing confidence in their reading. The F&P Text Level on the back cover serves as another tool to help you choose the right book for your child.

Remember, a lifetime love of reading starts with a single step!

To amazing stingrays everywhere
—C.G.

With special thanks to
Dr. Carl Luer and Mote Marine Laboratory
for their collaboration and guidance

Text copyright © 2015 by Carole Gerber
Illustrations copyright © 2015 by Isidre Mones

Photograph credits: Cover and pp. 8, 12, 34, 36 (top), 48: courtesy of Matt Weiss; p. 3: some rights reserved by Ed Schipul, found on Flickr Creative Commons; pp. 10–11, 13, 14–15, 37 (bottom), 38–39: courtesy of Phillip Colla; p. 10 (inset): some rights reserved by EpochCatcher, found on Flickr Creative Commons; pp. 30–31: some rights reserved by twodolla, found on Flickr Creative Commons; p. 36 (bottom): some rights reserved by prilfish, found on Flickr Creative Commons; p. 37 (top): some rights reserved by Amit Chattopadhyay, found on Flickr Creative Commons; p. 37 (middle): courtesy of Keri Wilk; pp. 44–45, 46–47: courtesy of Mote Marine Laboratory.

Visit us on the Web!
StepIntoReading.com
randomhousekids.com

Educators and librarians, for a variety of teaching tools, visit us at RHTeachersLibrarians.com

Library of Congress Cataloging-in-Publication Data
Gerber, Carole.
Stingrays! : underwater fliers / by Carole Gerber ; illustrated by Isidre Mones.
    pages   cm. — (Step into reading. Step 3)
Audience: Grades K–3.
ISBN 978-0-449-81308-9 (trade pbk.) — ISBN 978-0-375-97153-2 (lib. bdg.) —
ISBN 978-0-375-98142-5 (ebook)
1. Stingrays—Juvenile literature. I. Mones, Isidre, illustrator. II. Title.
    QL638.8.G47 2014   597.3'5—dc23   2013037897

Printed in the United States of America
10 9 8 7 6 5 4 3 2 1

This book has been officially leveled by using the F&P Text Level Gradient™ Leveling System.

Stingrays!

Underwater Fliers

by Carole Gerber

illustrations by Isidre Mones

Random House 🏠 New York

A hungry
southern stingray
hides on the seafloor.
She covers her flat,
boneless body with sand.

Other fish are hiding, too.

The stingray waits.

Something moves
under the sand.
Swish! Swish! Swish!
The stingray
uncovers a clam.

Plop! She drops
onto her prey.
The stingray's mouth
is on her underside.

She sucks up the clam.
Chomp! Chomp!
Her strong teeth
crush the shell.
She swallows the clam
and spits out the shell.

Now the stingray
is in danger!
A hammerhead shark
is on the hunt.
Sensors in its skin locate
the stingray.

Sensors

Sensors

Stingrays
also have sensors.
Sensors around the
stingray's mouth
detect that a shark
is nearby.

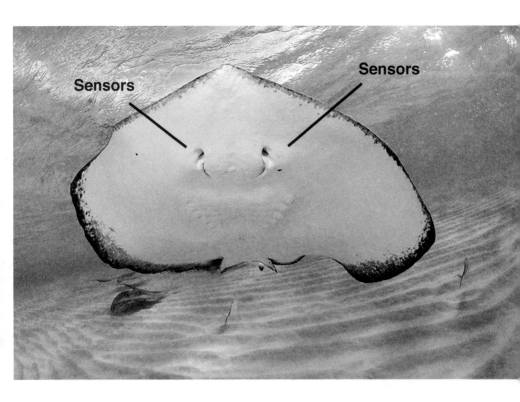

Sensors

Sensors

The stingray seems
to fly through the water.
Her fins move like wings.
She escapes!

The hammerhead
does not give up.
It loves to eat stingrays.
The shark swims
in big circles.

Soon it senses another
stingray buried
on the seafloor.
The shark uses its head
like a hammer.
It butts and pins down
a rough-tail stingray.

The rough-tail
fights back.
It raises its skinny tail.
Whack!

It drives in
a poisonous stinger,
or barb.
The barb breaks off
in the shark's mouth.
Ouch! It's sharp!

The hammerhead
has been stung before.
It ignores the pain.
It eats the rough-tail
in quick bites.

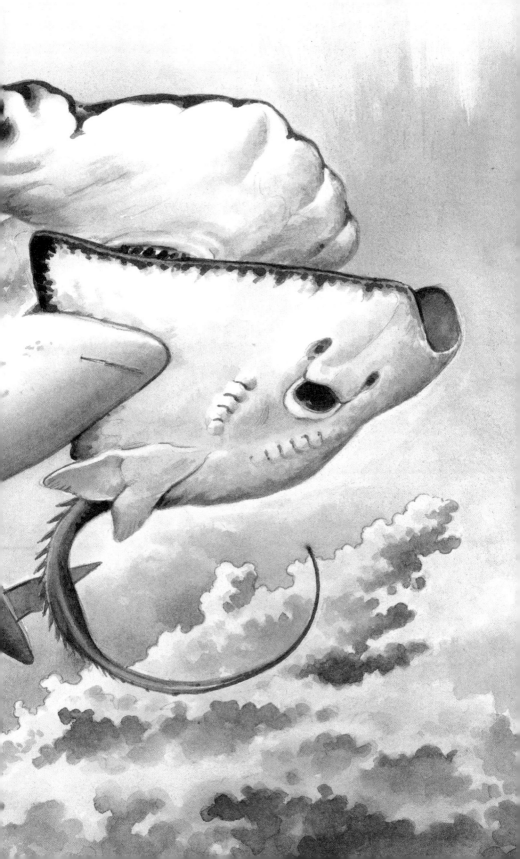

The southern stingray
got away just in time.
The eggs she is carrying
have hatched inside her.
Her babies, called pups,
come out of her body.
Look! There are seven.

The stingray

does not feed her pups.

They uncurl their fins

and swim away.

The pups may live

fifteen to twenty-five years.

Their mother swims away, too.
She goes to a place
where hogfish are waiting.
This area is called
a cleaning station.

She rests

as the hogfish eat the gunk

that coats her smooth skin.

The hogfish get fed.

The southern stingray

gets clean.

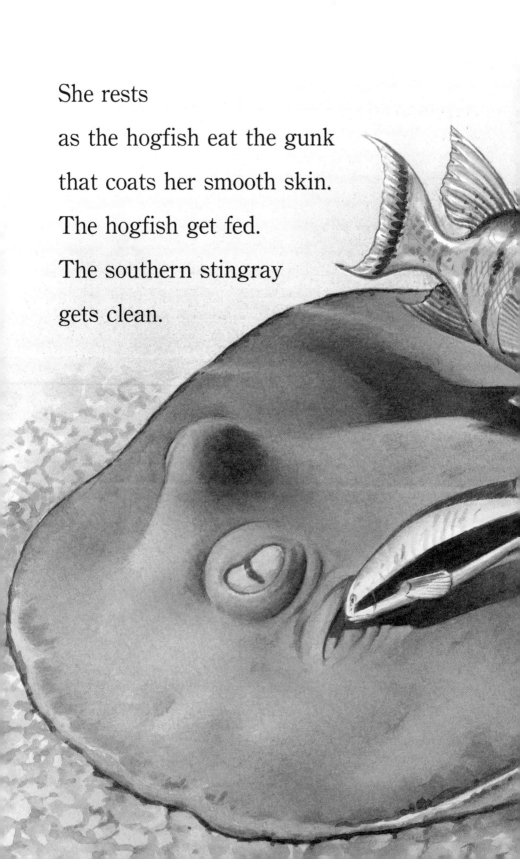

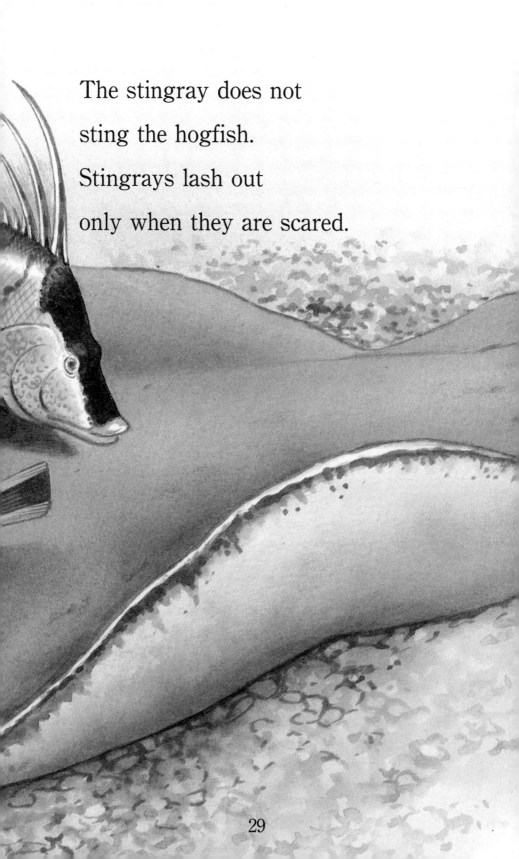

The stingray does not
sting the hogfish.
Stingrays lash out
only when they are scared.

Most stings occur
on feet and ankles.
Someone steps on
a stingray hiding in the sand.

To protect itself,
the stingray
lifts its tail.

Whap!
It drives in its stinger.
When the barb breaks the skin,
venom seeps
into the wound.
It hurts!

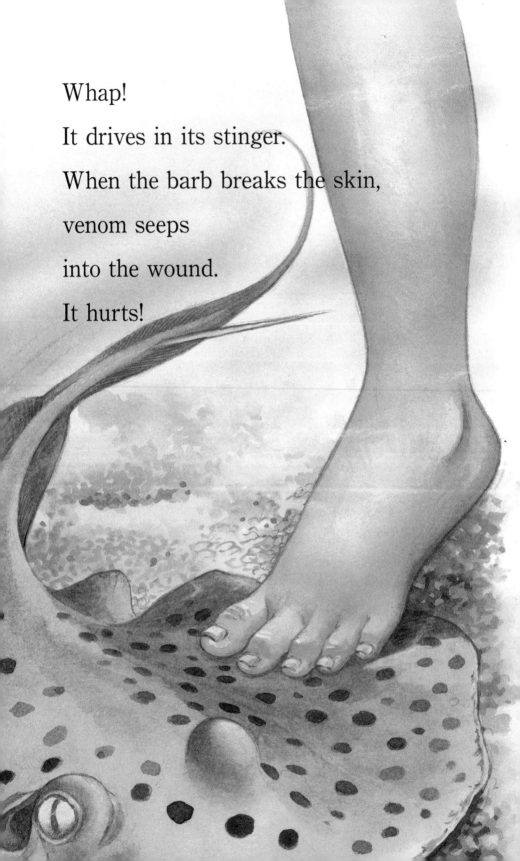

Victims of stings
need first aid.
The poison must
be washed from
the wound.
The barb must be
pulled out.

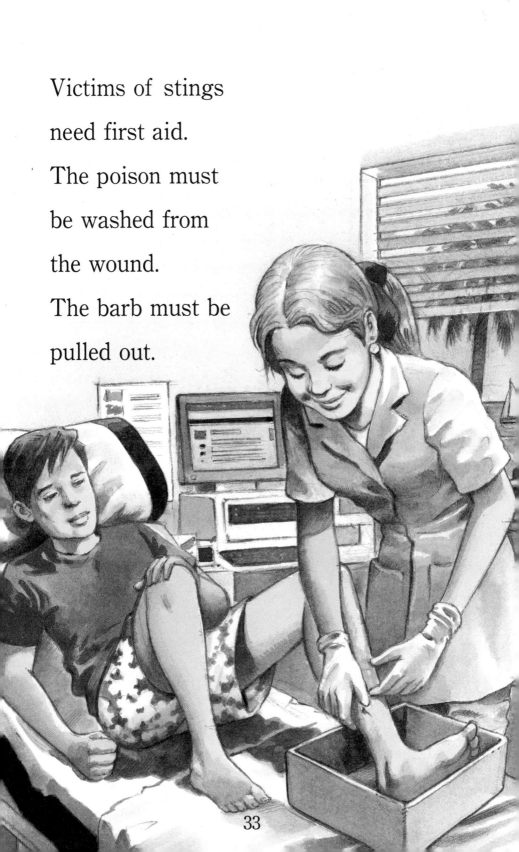

Luckily, stings rarely happen.

Stingrays are shy.

They tend to hide or swim away

from predators.

And they swim away fast!

How?

Because their skeletons
are made of cartilage.
So are your nose and ears.
Cartilage is soft,
and it bends.
Swimming stingrays
bend their fins like wings.
This is why they seem
to fly through the water.

There are hundreds
of kinds of stingrays!
They live in oceans
and in some rivers.

Some are drab,
like the southern
stingray.

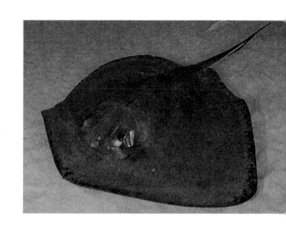

Some are bright,
like the ribbontail
stingray.

Some have long tails, like the whiptail stingray.

Some have stubby tails, like the short-tail stingray.

Some are small, like the yellow stingray.

Some are huge!
The manta ray
can grow to
thirty feet wide.

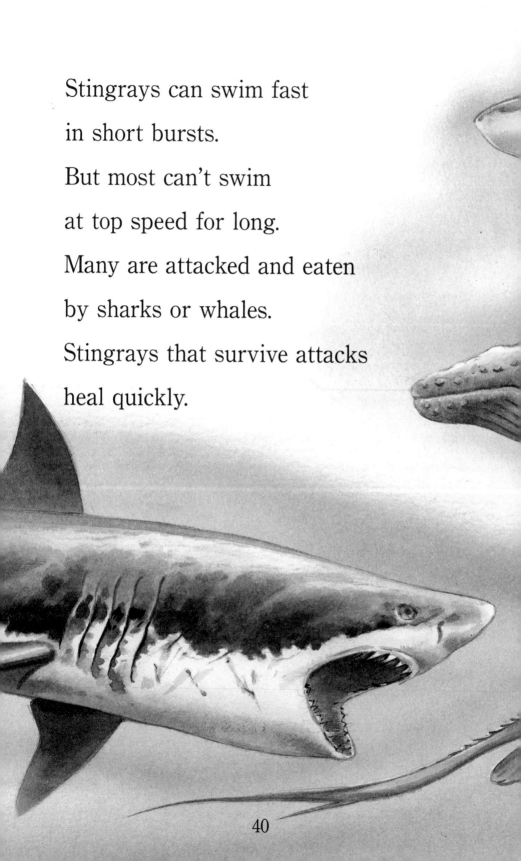

Stingrays can swim fast
in short bursts.
But most can't swim
at top speed for long.
Many are attacked and eaten
by sharks or whales.
Stingrays that survive attacks
heal quickly.

Scientists at Mote Marine Lab
in Sarasota, Florida,
want to learn why.
They believe that
good bacteria live
in the mucus that coats
stingrays' skin.

The scientists are
running tests
to see if the bacteria
can be used
to protect wounds
from infection.

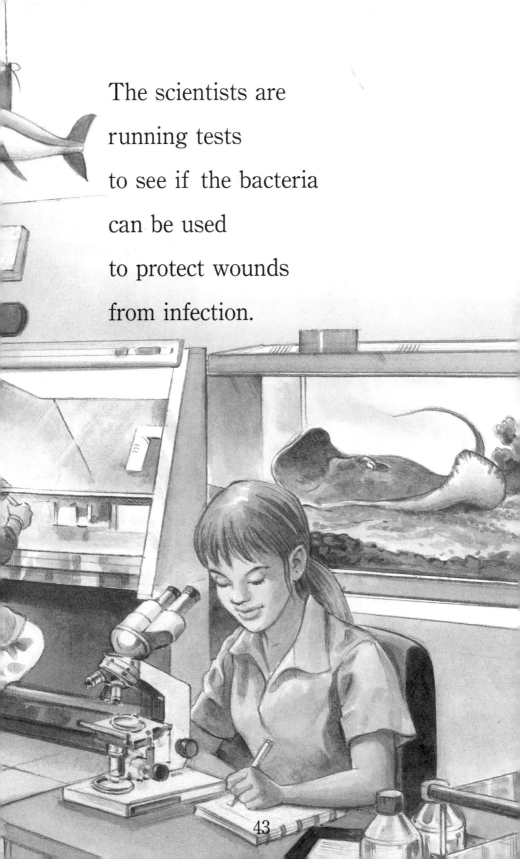

Mote Marine Lab also has

an aquarium.

Here, you can pet stingrays

placed in "ray trays."

For safety,
their stingers
have been removed.

Have you ever

touched a stingray?

Its skin is soft and slick.

The color of its skin
helps the stingray
blend into the sand.

Stingrays have lived
for millions of years.
Only a few kinds
are endangered.
These underwater fliers
will likely be around forever.

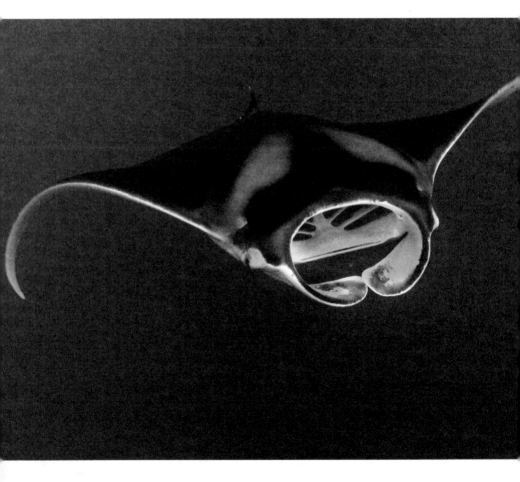